COELOPHYSIS

By Susan H. Gray

THE CHILD'S WORLD®
CHANHASSEN, MINNESOTA

The Child's World®

Published in the United States of America by The Child's World®
PO Box 326, Chanhassen, MN 55317-0326
800-599-READ
www.childsworld.com

Content Adviser:
Peter Makovicky,
Ph.D., Curator,
Field Museum,
Chicago, Illinois

Photo Credits: American Museum of Natural History: 10, 11, 17, 24; Corbis: 20
(Tim Davis), 23 (David Muench), 26 (Reuters NewMedia Inc.), 27 (James A. Sugar);
Douglas Henderson: 5, 6, 19, 21; Getty Images/Time Life Pictures/Bob Landry: 14, 16;
Mike Fredericks: 7; Photo Researchers: 9 (Kent & Donna Dannen), 25 (Science Photo
Library/Ludek Pesek); Photo Researchers/François Gohier: 13, 15; Visuals Unlimited/
Ken Lucas: 8.

The Child's World®: Mary Berendes, Publishing Director

Editorial Directions, Inc.: E. Russell Primm, Editorial Director; Ruth M. Martin, Line
Editor; Katie Marsico, Assistant Editor; Matthew Messbarger, Editorial Assistant; Susan
Hindman, Copy Editor; Susan Ashley, Proofreader; Tim Griffin, Indexer; Kerry Reid,
Fact Checker; Cian Loughlin O'Day, Photo Reseacher; Linda S. Koutris, Photo Selector

Original cover art by Todd Marshall

The Design Lab: Kathleen Petelinsek, Design and Art Direction; Kari Thornborough,
Page Production

Library of Congress Cataloging-in-Publication Data
Gray, Susan Heinrichs.
  Coelophysis / by Susan H. Gray.
     p. cm. — (Exploring dinosaurs)
Includes index.
Contents: Checking things out—What is a coelophysis?—Who found the first coelo-
physis?—What about the coelophysis bone bed?—More mysteries—Whatever became
of coelophysis?
  ISBN 1-59296-185-1 (lib. bdg. : alk. paper)
  1. Coelophysis—Juvenile literature. [1. Coelophysis. 2. Dinosaurs.] I. Title. II. Series.
QE862.S3G693 2004
567.912—dc22   2003018624

Table of Contents

CHAPTER ONE

CHECKING THINGS OUT

Little *Coelophysis* (SEE-loe-FY-siss) and his brother were checking things out. They were only a year old and full of energy. It was a great day. The sun was shining. The air was fresh. Ferns swayed in the breeze.

Suddenly, something green flashed across the ground. The brothers spun around to see it. They stood perfectly still, barely breathing. Zip! There it was again—skittering over a rock and out of sight.

The brothers wasted no time and darted after the little lizard. They stopped before a big clump of ferns and peered between the leaves. They reached underneath the plants and felt around on the ground. Nothing. The lizard was gone.

Coelophysis was a theropod with a body about the size of a turkey's. Theropods were carnivorous dinosaurs with strong hind legs and small arms. Some scientists think that theropods are the ancestors of birds.

Then, in the distance, they heard a familiar sound. It was the

other members of their herd—and they were making quite a racket.

One big *Coelophysis* was chomping on a dinosaur he had just killed.

His fellow hunters were tearing apart three others.

Hunting in a pack would have given this small dinosaur an advantage when making a kill. Alone, a Coelophysis *may have been a match only for small mammals and reptiles. Many* Coelophysis *hunting together would have been able to take down much larger prey.*

All the members of the herd gathered around the **prey.** Claws

ripped at the fresh meat. Powerful jaws crunched on bones. One

Coelophysis shoved her head inside a **carcass** and tore out a mouth-

ful of flesh. The little brothers completely forgot about the lizard.

It was lunchtime!

CHAPTER TWO

WHAT IS A COELOPHYSIS?

Coelophysis is a dinosaur that lived from about 225 million to 208 million years ago. Its name is taken from Greek words that mean "hollow form." The name refers to the hollow, lightweight bones of the **reptile.**

Coelophysis was among the first dinosaurs to walk the Earth. It was a slender animal, about 10 feet (3 meters) long. Its tail was about the same length as the rest of its body. It had a long, narrow head and a large mouth filled with

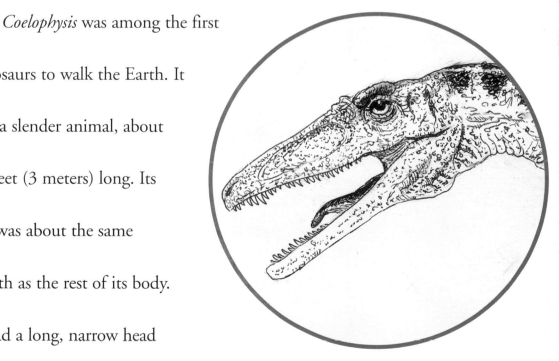

Armed with an uncommonly large brain in its small head, the Coelophysis *was well equipped to out think almost all other dinosaurs of the late Triassic period.*

This fossilized Coelophysis *skeleton shows the dinosaur's slender body.* Coelophysis *fossils have been found in New Mexico, Utah, Arizona, and Texas. Close relatives of the dinosaur have been found as far away as Australia!*

sharp teeth. Its neck was long and flexible. An adult weighed between 40 and 70 pounds (18 and 32 kilograms).

Coelophysis had short, strong arms. Each hand had three fingers, and each finger was armed with a sharp claw. The hands and claws were good for grasping other animals and tearing them apart.

The dinosaur's legs were slender and muscular. Each foot ended with three long, clawed toes. When standing up on its back legs, *Coelophysis* was about 4 feet (1.2 m) tall. The dinosaur probably walked on two legs most of the time. With its strong legs and light bones, *Coelophysis* was probably a fast runner.

JUST WHAT IS A FOSSIL?

We know that *Coelophysis* existed because scientists have found its fossils. Fossils are the remains of ancient living things. They are the clues that tell us about plants and animals from millions of years ago. Most fossils left by *Coelophysis* are its bones, claws, and teeth.

There are different kinds of fossils. Some fossils are actually left-over parts of plants and animals. For instance, animal body parts like bones, teeth, scales, shells, and horns are often found as fossils. These are called body fossils. Usually, the hard-est body parts of an animal become fossilized.

Plants also leave pieces of themselves behind. Flowering plants make a fine, grainy material called pollen (PAWL-un). Fossilized pollen is sometimes found right alongside a fossilized animal skeleton. Scientists study the pollen to learn what kinds of

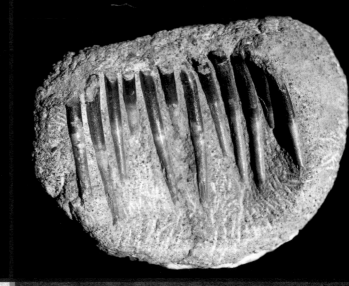

plants lived in that animal's environment.

Ancient plants and animals left other kinds of fossils behind, too. These are not actual parts of those plants and animals. But they give us clues that these things existed. Such fossils are called trace fossils. They include footprints, nests, and burrows.

Some things in nature look like fossils, but they are not fossils at all. These are called pseudofossils (SOO-doe-FOSS-ulz). Pseudo comes from a Greek word that means "fake" or "false." People are often fooled by these objects. Pseudofossils could be large, smooth, round rocks that look like dinosaur eggs. They could be holes that look like animal tunnels. They might even be rocks with stains that look just like ferns.

Scientists who study fossils and ancient life are called paleontologists (PAY-lee-un-TAWL-uh-jists). They learn to tell real fossils from pseudofossils. But sometimes pseudofossils even trick the experts.

CHAPTER THREE

WHO FOUND THE
FIRST *COELOPHYSIS?*

In 1881, a fossil hunter named David Baldwin found the first

Coelophysis remains. Baldwin worked for a famous paleontolo-

gist named Edward

Drinker Cope. As a pa-

leontologist, Cope often

led teams of scientists on

fossil-hunting trips. Many

of his trips were quite suc-

cessful. His teams spread

out across large areas and

picked through rocks for

days. They found plenty of

Edward Drinker Cope was born in 1840 and was responsible for naming about 1,000 species of fossil animals over the course of his lifetime. The discovery of Coelophysis *is considered to be one of the most important dinosaur finds ever made.*

fossils and discovered many new dinosaurs. One of the teams

included David Baldwin. But rather than work with a large group

of people, Baldwin liked to work alone.

One day, he was out fossil hunting in New Mexico. He came

across some little bones that were different from others he had

seen before. The bones were from the legs, back, hips, and ribs

of some kind of animal. He picked up as many bones as he could,

then sent them to his boss, Mr. Cope. After studying the bones

for several years, Cope decided that this was a new dinosaur and

that its name should be *Coelophysis.*

Not much happened with *Coelophysis* during the next 60

years. Scientists did not have many fossils to study, so they could

not learn much about the dinosaur's life. Then, in 1947, another

fossil hunter named Edwin Colbert was exploring in New Mexico

According to the National Dinosaur Museum, the first Spanish settlers in New Mexico believed Los Brujos—*the area where Baldwin discovered* Coelophysis—*was haunted by ghostly "serpents."*

with some of his friends.

They knew that David

Baldwin had found

Coelophysis fossils in the

area years earlier, and they

wanted to see if there were

others. One day, they found

a few bones at the bottom

of a hill.

They started chipping

After his breakthrough discovery in New Mexico, Edwin Colbert (left) went on to find the first Antarctic dinosaur fossil—a Lystrosaurus.

away the dirt and rocks, and

more bones appeared. The men decided to keep at it until they

found everything they could. In time, they chipped away the entire

hill! But the work was worth it. Underneath the hill was one of the greatest fossil finds ever. The men had uncovered hundreds of

Coelophysis skeletons, and many were in great shape. Now scien-

tists had plenty of material to study.

The Coelophysis *skeletons Colbert's team found were a very important discovery.*
They helped scientists gain a better understanding of all theropods.

WHAT DO BONE BEDS TELL US?

Edwin Colbert and his friends had discovered a *Coelophysis* bone bed. A bone bed is a group of many skeletons found in one place. There are several ways that bone beds might have formed.

Perhaps a group of dinosaurs lived together in a herd, then all died at about the same time. Their skeletons could be preserved together as one large bone bed. Or perhaps several dinosaurs died alone and in separate places. Then a flood washed their bodies down to the same area. Their

skeletons, too, might form a bone bed.

It is possible that meat-eating dinosaurs dragged their prey home to a nest. After eating the meat, they would leave the bones of their meal scattered nearby. Millions of years later, scientists might discover this area and call it a bone bed. They might think these were the bones of a herd of dinosaurs, even though the truth was far different.

Scientists think long and hard before they decide what caused a bone bed. They know that not all bone beds are from herding animals. If a bone bed contains just one kind of dinosaur, they think the dinosaur *might* have lived in a herd. If they find more bone beds with just that same dinosaur, this is more proof that it lived in a herd. And if they find bone beds with babies, youngsters, and adults of just that dinosaur, they are almost certain it lived in a herd.

CHAPTER FOUR

WHAT ABOUT THE COELOPHYSIS BONE BED?

The *Coelophysis* bone bed was loaded with skeletons. Some bones were heaped together. Other skeletons looked perfectly undisturbed.

While the bones told paleontologists a lot about the little dinosaur, they also raised some big questions. Was there more than one kind of *Coelophysis?* Did *Coelophysis* really live in a big herd? Why? What did all of those dinosaurs eat?

It was not unusual for some dinosaurs to live in herds. After all, there was safety in a herd. A few members could watch for danger while the others ate. Adult dinosaurs could guard the younger ones. **Predatory** dinosaurs could hunt by ganging up on their prey. Many modern animals live in herds and do these things, so why not *Coelophysis?*

One theory about the Coelophysis *bone bed suggests that hundreds of these dinosaurs were drawn to the banks of a nearby river as large numbers of fish began to mate. An unexpected and violent storm could have caused flash flooding, drowning all of the unlucky* Coelophysis *that had taken advantage of the free meal.*

At first, the *Coelophysis* bone bed seemed to prove that the

dinosaurs did live in huge groups. But then scientists gave it more

thought. Modern animals that live in big herds are herbivores

(URB-uh-vores). They eat only plants. They slowly roam from place to place, chewing up leaves and grasses. But *Coelophysis* was a carnivore (KAR-nih-vore). It dined only on meat. Modern carnivores either live alone or in small groups or packs, not in huge herds.

Now, scientists aren't so sure about how the dinosaur lived. They don't know why all of those skeletons ended up together.

Some modern-day animals, including wolves, are known for living in packs. Wolves are one of the most highly social of all carnivores. Packs often exist to make hunting more effective and to give pack members more protection.

At the close of the Triassic period, a large meteorite struck the northeastern region of present-day Canada. This catastrophe is thought to have caused the extinction of many species and might have killed the dinosaurs whose remains make up the Coelophysis *bone bed.*

Maybe a lot of *Coelophysis* died of starvation. Then a huge flood

might have collected all their skeletons and piled them up. Perhaps

the animals died during a **drought.** Scientists aren't even sure if

all the *Coelophysis* in the bone bed died at the same time.

CHAPTER FIVE

MORE MYSTERIES

The bone bed in New Mexico clearly contained *Coelophysis* skeletons. The skeletons had the long necks, toothy mouths, three-fingered hands, and three-toed feet of *Coelophysis.* But when scientists looked closer, they saw some big differences.

Some adults had more slender bones than others. They were probably slim dinosaurs. Other adults had sturdier bones. These probably came from larger more powerful dinosaurs.

Some scientists believe that the skeletons came from two different kinds of *Coelophysis.* The two kinds might have lived in the same area. Their living spaces may have overlapped. Other scientists think the skeletons are all from the same kind of *Coelophysis.* The different bone types could be from males and

Today, differences in size between males and females can be seen among many birds and reptiles. Perhaps male Coelophysis were larger than female Coelophysis. Or the females could have been larger than the males.

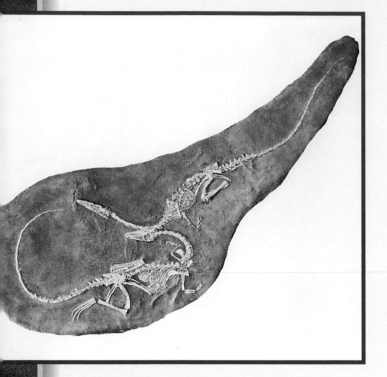

This fossil displays the remains of two Coelophysis. Coelophysis *probably existed from the late Triassic period until the early Jurassic period. That means the* Coelophysis *lived more than 200 million years ago!*

females. This question might never be settled.

There is another mystery surrounding *Coelophysis*. Some of the adult fossils found in the bone bed seemed to have little *Coelophysis* skeletons inside of them. This could mean the dinosaur was a cannibal! When food was scarce, it might have eaten younger members of its own herd. After all, this happens among some carnivores of today.

But maybe it wasn't cannibal after all. Some scientists believe the adult skeletons just happen to lie on top of the baby skeletons. Again, we may never know the answer.

CHAPTER SIX

WHATEVER BECAME OF *COELOPHYSIS?*

No one is certain why any of the dinosaurs, including *Coelophysis,* died out. The small size, speed, and hunting methods of *Coelophysis* helped it survive for millions of years. But something caused the little dinosaur to disappear. What could it have been?

This is the sort of question that puzzles paleontologists. There were hundreds of different kinds of dinosaurs. Many of them were

This is what scientists think Earth looked like in the Triassic period, when Coelophysis *existed. Temperatures were probably very warm, and evergreen trees made up much of the plant life. Dinosaurs first appeared during the late Triassic period.*

Paleontologists are still discovering, excavating, and preserving new dinosaur bones today. Pale-ontologists are like detectives. They uncover clues that help them to solve the puzzles of the past.

around for millions of years. So they must have been pretty

good survivors. Still, something caused them to die out complete-

ly. When one kind of animal totally disappears, it is said to be

extinct (ex-TINGKT).

It is hard to know what caused an ancient animal to become

extinct. To figure it out, scientists study the rocks from the ani-

mal's area and time period. Sometimes rocks will show whether a lot

of volcanoes were erupting when the animal died out. Rocks can offer clues as to the gases in the environment. Rocks can also show if there was flooding at the time.

So far, though, no one has figured out exactly what killed *Coelophysis.* No one is even sure what killed the dinosaurs in the *Coelophysis* bone bed. It seems that the more we study dinosaurs, the more questions we have!

Paleontologists use many different kinds of tools—both big and small. From hammers and shovels, to brushes and tweezers, these tools help them recognize and uncover fossils that are millions of years old.

Glossary

ancient (AYN-shunt) Something that is ancient is very old; from millions of years ago. Paleontology is the study of ancient plant and animal life.

carcass (KAR-kuhss) A carcass is the body of a dead animal. A meat-eating dinosaur would kill an animal and then eat parts of its carcass.

drought (DROWT) A drought is a long period of dry weather. A drought might kill a group of animals because they cannot find enough to drink.

environment (en-VYE-ruhn-muhnt) An environment is made up of the things that surround a living creature, such as the air and soil. Prehistoric rocks offer clues about what gases existed in the environment when *Coelophysis* lived.

fossilized (FOSS-uhl-eyezed) Something that is fossilized became a fossil. Paleontologists study the fossilized parts of plants and animals.

predatory (PRED-uh-tor-ee) An animal is predatory if it hunts and eats other animals. *Coelophysis* was a predatory dinosaur.

prey (PRAY) Prey are animals that are hunted and eaten by other animals. Scientists think that *Coelophysis* used its sharp claws to tear its prey apart.

reptile (REP-tile) A reptile is an air-breathing animal with a backbone and is usually covered with scales or plates. *Coelophysis* was a reptile.

Did You Know?

▸ *Coelophysis* is the state fossil of New Mexico.

▸ *Coelophysis* was about as tall and as heavy as a third-grade student of today.

▸ In 1998, a *Coelophysis* skull traveled with astronauts on a space shuttle trip.

The Geologic Time Scale

TRIASSIC PERIOD

Date: 248 million to 208 million years ago

Fossils: *Coelophysis, Cynodont, Desmatosuchus, Eoraptor, Gerrothorax, Peteinosaurus, Placerias, Plateosaurus, Postosuchus, Procompsognathus, Riojasaurus, Saltopus, Teratosaurus, Thecodontosaurus*

Distinguishing Features: For the most part, the climate in the Triassic period was hot and dry. The first true mammals appeared during this period, as well as turtles, frogs, salamanders, and lizards. Corals could also be found in oceans at this time, although large reefs such as the ones we have today did not yet exist. Evergreen trees made up much of the plant life.

JURASSIC PERIOD

Date: 208 million to 144 million years ago

Fossils: *Allosaurus, Anchisaurus, Apatosaurus, Barosaurus, Brachiosaurus, Ceratosaurus, Compsognathus, Cryptoclidus, Dilophosaurus, Diplodocus, Eustreptospondylus, Hybodus, Janenschia, Kentrosaurus, Liopleurodon, Megalosaurus, Opthalmosaurus, Rhamphorhynchus, Saurolophus, Segisaurus, Seismosaurus, Stegosaurus, Supersaurus, Syntarsus, Ultrasaurus, Vulcanodon, Xiaosaurus*

Distinguishing Features: The climate of the Jurassic period was warm and moist. The first birds appeared during this period. Plant life was also greener and more widespread. Sharks began swimming in Earth's oceans. Although dinosaurs didn't even exist at the beginning of the Triassic period, they ruled Earth by Jurassic times. There was a minor mass extinction toward the end of the Jurassic period.

CRETACEOUS PERIOD

Date: 144 million to 65 million years ago

Fossils: *Acrocanthosaurus, Alamosaurus, Albertosaurus, Anatotitan, Ankylosaurus, Argentinosaurus, Bagaceratops, Baryonyx, Carcharodontosaurus, Carnotaurus, Centrosaurus, Chasmosaurus, Corythosaurus, Didelphodon, Edmontonia, Edmontosaurus, Gallimimus, Gigantosaurus, Hadrosaurus, Hypsilophodon, Iguanodon, Kronosaurus, Lambeosaurus, Leaellynasaura, Maiasaura, Megaraptor, Muttaburrasaurus, Nodosaurus, Ornithocheirus, Oviraptor, Pachycephalosaurus, Panoplosaurus, Parasaurolophus, Pentaceratops, Polacanthus, Protoceratops, Psittacosaurus, Quaesitosaurus, Saltasaurus, Sarcosuchus, Saurolophus, Sauropelta, Saurornithoides, Segnosaurus, Spinosaurus, Stegoceras, Stygimoloch, Styracosaurus, Tapejara, Tarbosaurus, Therizinosaurus, Thescelosaurus, Torosaurus, Trachodon, Triceratops, Troodon, Tyrannosaurus rex, Utahraptor, Velociraptor*

Distinguishing Features: The climate of the Cretaceous period was fairly mild. Flowering plants first appeared in this period, and many modern plants developed. With flowering plants came a greater diversity of insect life. Birds further developed into two types: flying and flightless. A wider variety of mammals also existed. At the end of this period came a great mass extinction that wiped out the dinosaurs, along with several other groups of animals.

How to Learn More

At the Library

Gillette, J. Lynett, and Douglas Henderson (illustrator). *Dinosaur Ghosts: The Mystery of Coelophysis.* New York: Dial Books for Young Readers, 1997.

Lambert, David, Darren Naish, and Liz Wyse. *Dinosaur Encyclopedia.* New York: DK Publishing, 2001.

Palmer, Douglas, Colin Harrison, Barry Cox, R. J. G. Savage, and Brian Gardiner. *The Simon & Schuster Encyclopedia of Dinosaurs and Prehistoric Creatures: A Visual Who's Who of Prehistoric Life.* New York: Simon & Schuster, 1999.

On the Web

Visit our home page for lots of links about *Coelophysis:*
http://www.childsworld.com/links.html
Note to Parents, Teachers, and Librarians: We routinely verify our
Web links to make sure they're safe, active sites—so encourage
your readers to check them out!

Places to Visit or Contact

AMERICAN MUSEUM OF NATURAL HISTORY
*To view numerous dinosaur fossils, as well
as the fossils of several ancient mammals*
Central Park West at 79th Street
New York, NY 10024-5192
212/769-5100

CARNEGIE MUSEUM OF NATURAL HISTORY
To see a Coelophysis *skull and a cast of an entire* Coelophysis *skeleton*
4400 Forbes Avenue
Pittsburgh, PA 15213
412/622-3131

DINOSAUR NATIONAL MONUMENT
To view a huge deposit of dinosaur bones in a natural setting
Dinosaur, CO 81610-9724
or
Dinosaur National Monument (Quarry)
11625 East 1500 South
Jensen, UT 84035
435/781-7700

MUSEUM OF THE ROCKIES
To see real dinosaur fossils, as well as robotic replicas
Montana State University
600 West Kagy Boulevard
Bozeman, MT 59717-2730
406/994-2251 or 406/994-DINO (3466)

NATIONAL MUSEUM OF NATURAL HISTORY
(SMITHSONIAN INSTITUTION)
To see several dinosaur exhibits and special behind-the-scenes tours
10th Street and Constitution Avenue, N.W.
Washington, D.C. 20560-0166
202/357-2700

Index

About the Author

Susan H. Gray has bachelor's and master's degrees in zoology, and has taught college-level courses in biology. She first fell in love with fossil hunting while studying paleontology in college. In her 25 years as an author, she has written many articles for scientists and researchers, and many science books for children. Susan enjoys gardening, traveling, and playing the piano. She and her husband, Michael, live in Cabot, Arkansas.